Hand on the Navel

Hand on the Navel

Lemuel Johnson

Africa World Press, Inc.

P.O. Box 1892
Trenton, New Jersey 08607

Africa World Press, Inc.
P.O. Box 1892
Trenton, NJ 08607

Book and Cover Design: Carles J. Juzang

Library of Congress Cataloging-in-Publication Data

Johnson, Lemuel A.
    Hand on the Navel / Lemuel Johnson.
       p. cm.
    ISBN 0-86543-484-0 (Hdbk.). -- ISBN 0-86543-485-9
    1. Great Britain, Army. Royal West African Frontier Force-
-Poetry. 2. Soldiers--Africa Western--Poetry. 3. World War,
1914-1918--Poetry. 4. World War, 1939-1945--Poetry. I. Title.
PR9393.9.J6H3   1995
821--dc20   95-142
                                                 CIP

For Marian for Yma & for Yshélu

Research into and production of *The Sierra Leone Trilogy* benefitted from assistance provided by the University of Michigan's Graduate School and by the Offices of the Vice Provosts for Research and for Academic and Multicultural Affairs.

CONTENTS

Introduction to the Sierra Leone Trilogy

"How To Breathe Dead Hippo Meat, and Live" ix

I. The Book of Corporal Bundu, RWAFF

Prologue 5
Part I... 8
Part II.. 10
Part III 17
Part IV 23
Part V: Armistice 31

II. Vademecum

Requiem for a lapsed catholic.. 45
Postmortem for a resurrectionist 48
Compline 49
Caribbean sugar... 50

III. Swagger sticks

Conversion of the ethiopian eunuch 53
Short visit to Auschwitz 54
A celebration in Istanbul.. 55
Orfeo, with his lute 56
Calypso for Caliban 58

IV. Circular ruins

The idea of jumping 65
Sufi: tariqa 66
With a knife or razor blade... 67
Funeral rites 68
The growing of grapes 69
Belladonna 70
Armistice 71

Notes 73

■ ■ ■ ■ ■ ■ ■ ■ ■

How To Breathe Dead Hippo Meat, and Live

*[The coercions and conversions of exile eventually gener-
ate something] like a do-it-yourself kit, with which to forge
identity: signs, symbols, language bits of quote, fragments of
allusive references, clusters of associations, sounds and the
structuring of sounds with which to fabricate a biography.*
Sylvia Wynter, "Afterword," ***Highlife for Caliban.***

*The earth for us is a place to live in, where we must put up
with sights, with sounds, with smells, too, by Jove!—breathe
dead hippo, so to speak, and not be contaminated.*
Jozef Teodor Konrad Korzeniowski, (aka Joseph
Conrad: born December 3, 1857 Bedichev, Poland, now in
the Ukraine; died 1924, Canterbury, Kent, England—in his
identity as great English novelist of imperialist adventures,
particularly those of Belgium's King Leopold II in the very heart
of darkness).

Henrietta Street, London, England, makes for a starting
point that is as implausible as it may be said to be unavoid-
able, given the oddly syncopated rhythms of our "high life."
In *The Mysterious Mr. Eliot*, a biographical documentary about
the St. Louis-born, USA writer, turned High Anglican and High
Modernist English poet, one of the persons interviewed
recalls a visit to T.S. Eliot's desk when he was employed at
Lloyd's Bank: "There he was, poor man, *the* poet of our time,
adding up figures in a bank." And all day the heels of pass-
ersby went *clok clok, clok clok* six inches overhead, on the
pavement of Henrietta Street. Such bits of information, at
once useful and exotically pointless—very much like dead
hippo meat, perhaps—do have a way of developing into criti-
cal noises in one's head. In the event, my being thus crossed
up at and into Henrietta Street may not have been altogether
that odd, or unproductive. For I happened upon Henrietta
Street at about the same time, in the 1970s, that I embarked
upon the three-volume poetry sequence that would culmi-
nate in *Carnival of the Old Coast*. To explain further the coin-
cidence of dislocation and inspiration that the Sierra Leone
trilogy has since worked to contain, I borrow from George

Lamming's *The Pleasures of Exile* what amounts to a mani-festo and poetics of exile: "The pleasure [and] the paradox of...exile is that I belong wherever I am. My role, it seems, has rather to do with time and change than with the geogra-phy of circumstances; and yet there is an acre of ground in the New World which keeps growing echoes in my head. I can only hope that these echoes do not die before my work comes to an end" (1992: 50).

After a rather extended stay away from Sierra Leone, my concern in the poetry trilogy was to return in a way that would recover the years from the 1500s to the 1960s; and to do so by way of a strategic deployment of contexts in my Sierra Leone Krio heritage. I decided then that I would focus on the remarkably elastic features of this culture's peculiar history of scatteration and re-grouping. In brief, the volumes, *Highlife for Caliban* (1940s-1960s), *Hand on the Navel* (1914-1945), and *Carnival of the Old Coast* (1500s-1950s), would ride out and into the various filiations and languages of Sierra Leone's creolization. The sequence would thus negotiate its way, traffic and trade, if necessary, into a complex cultural genealogy; a genealogy that is as much Yoruba as it is Afro-Brazilian Por-tuguese; as much Liverpool and Hull as Nova Scotia and Jamaican Maroon. The product, too, of the coast of the Caro-linas as well as of the Gullah islands, the trilogy would be as answerable to its ancestry in Afro-Christian *shout* as it would be to the call of the Afro-Islamic Aku Krio concentration at Fourah Bay, in the east end of Freetown. An item in *The Sierra Leone Weekly News* of December 20, 1902 rather elaborately understood such an arrangement of lines of suc-cession to mean that "being a Creole or Sierra Leonean [could] not be a nationality; it is an act of grace."

In the trilogy the attendant signs and wonders of such a view are used to re-fashion, "make personal," what I had already explored in the over-arching concerns of *The Devil, the Gargoyle and the Buffoon*. There, the preoccupation had been with studying how and why various shades of "negro," of "blackness-in-human-form," have been invariably served up in painfully assaultive representations. The relevant con-texts had been engaged in any number of national litera-tures. Circumstance and incident ranged accordingly: from the South Pacific of Captain Cook to the near finality of Germany's *Schrecklichkeit* (1904-1907) solution for the Hereros, under the Great Kaiser and his General Von Trotha.

Tracing these forms of denigration also led one from the romantic extravagance of Victor Hugo to the seemingly unmotivated malice of Shakespeare's Iago; from the grandly Prussian anxieties of the philosopher Oswald Spengler to the *tremendista* sensuality of Ramon del Valle-Inclan and his view of "un negro colossal" in the *Sonatas: Memorias del Marques de Bradomin* (1959).

The poetry volumes have sought to "thicken" with historical edge and sensuous detail the export and the import of such encounters—as happens, in "Giddy Appetites," among the "scholars," as we were called, of the Sierra Leone Grammar School Choir (1956-1958):

The song cycles are done.
they have gone quiet, the quinqueremes
of Ninevah, row their way
home, and become nothing to us.

I slip down a morning peculiar
to this coast; freighted with gold bits,
salt, really, paraquay tea; these
nine books for buenos ayres; a like
a parcel of guinea grain and negro
sails with us, weighs with us into port.

oigame, y que dios nos bendiga
and for those stately spanish galleons
too, remember, that made
brightness and bone structure a puzzle
in apes and peacocks for us.

still, that children never know
the measure and the full
beat of things, or learn too
well the native shift of difference
in the unquiet privilege of song
        —all this means nothing;
we were, after all, smaller
then than the disfiguring joke.
we were giddy so with appetite.
we could hold so to notes played
out beyond even the tenor of our days.

Within other cartographies, the poetry volumes have sought out the implications for Krenakore Brazil and for the Africa of "queen Victoria days" and its wars; for Aborigine Australia and along the sidewalk cafes of the Cours Mirabeau, in Aix-en-Provence where I had received some university training in European art and architecture. So, too, riding the trains from Paris to Venice, by way of Florence, when "the train clattered out of Milan/and the men, inside our compartment,/ [scratched] so at their groins." I recall now that *i signiori veneziani* flogged their forefingers so inside the palm of the hand, "wondering how well you (blonde of hair) and I 'did it.'"

there are fishhbones in Venice,
too, and the screams of urgent cats
and small streets they call Pavarotti.
water sucks at the rotting stones of our hotel.

we do not give birth with ease
here...

Just as relevant were memories of mosques with long-jointed minarets along the Niger and Benue Rivers in Nigeria. These memories led to the foregrounding of twelfth-century islamic cultures, and their making of black eunuchs for caliphs and harems. For when the unmaking of such men was not the case in North Africa, it was so, for sure, in the thousand and one nights of Persia and of "Arabia Felix"—in places with "names jingling so like oases/and jewels on a golddark belly;" where,

by the hill of Arafa, once,
Abraham, peace be upon him, stoned
the devil in his anger, not in ours;

we who can contain no such
history of hell; why, after all,
should fine silk be friend to wool?

"You can't breathe dead hippo meat waking, sleeping, and eating, and at the same time keep your precarious grip on existence," says Korzeniowski-Conrad's Marlow, when he is caught in the act of being very nearly at impossible odds with himself, in the very heart of his darkness. True enough, I should think. Which is why *Highlife for Caliban* moved to

record its own calculus of allegiance and vision, by a re-sit-
ing of Henrietta Street in a poem titled "Letter to My Tailor"—
because, "lately, I have taken to trousers/with buttons on a
long fly; being/lately, in no hurry to ease myself;"

> lately, I have taken to walking,
> here, with my elbows close to my body.
>
> if you like, you may say,
> I do not like the climate, or, again
> you may say, if you like, you may say
> "this one has taken twelve stitches inside
> the corners of his mouth; his elbows,
> now, keep the rebellion in his brittle bones polite."

In one of its meanings, *highlife* is a West African dance.
And the elbow-room movements to which this Caliban thus
devotes his attention have much in common with all those
back-to-the-native land steps that Martinique's Aimé Césaire,
for one, had so decisively played out in *Cahier d'un retour au
pays natal,* in 1939. As things turn out, the "elbow-room"
poems of *Highlife* recalculate the weight of ideas, and the
invitations, that appear on sale, or merely on display, along
the Henrietta Streets of our various exiles—whether they are
hung up for the lower reach of Tarzan and television, or in
the no doubt higher academic ambitiousness of Marx and
Aristotle; of Hegel, Ortega y Gasset, and other "disinterested
contemplations of the human experience." In either case,
subsequent shifts in the valuing of high life, or low, coalesce
in the elbow-room anxieties of the class of "we" that gets to
speak in "Exorcism":

> narrow
> as a calvinist's ark
> this, too,
> is the place
> built for us
> by strangers...
>
> why else
> would old photographs
> turn yellow
> against the walls?

why else
would glass
refuse
our reflection
turning
to the wall?

And in the *ora pro nobis* segments of "Calypso for Caliban" a similar play of refusal and refraction determines the burden of Caliban's recognition of what happens "when I set down so to substance/and to sum, but, seduced, think/to be elf with printless foot/is admiration and nice."

No doubt, one of the perquisites of Power is the capacity to determine when and how and if one's Truth can have Universal weight. Naturally, I oppose the heft and muscle of such capital-letter formations to the parochial density of folk who can be ever so easily pushed outside History. The capacity to stand, bulwarked, against the subversive penetration of strangers does have its advantages. So, too, are there disadvantages to being (always and only) problematically available for assimilation. This is especially the case for participant-outsiders, for *gastarbeiter* folk, if you wish. It is peculiarly so, I would think, for the alien(ated) who are, or see themselves as, permanently exiled from native clusters where the sanction of citizenship is legitimized into the comfort and power of belonging. The cluster of effects is succinctly captured when Ralph Ellison's Invisible Man points to the existential weightlessness of it all: "Outside the Brotherhood, we were outside history; but inside it they didn't see us. It was a hell of a state of affairs."

The roles that exile-participants assume under these circumstances invite comparisons. One such role is that of the model Alien/Visitor/Guest Worker. And here, one might think of, say, Othello in Venice, *before* his assumptions about the degree to which Desdemona is available. All the same, close encounters of the model kind may be offered, and sustained, with decorum and apparent good grace. Therefrom might emerge a kind of Naipaulian Exile-as-Honorary-Gentleman. Still, the honorific status could become urgent—modulating to The Exile as Noble, *and Necessary*, Moor. Necessary because, as in the case of Othello when we meet him, truly illegal aliens, as constituted in the likes of infidel/uncircumcized Turk/moslem *Ausländer*, are already within shooting distance of Venice, and shooting. Fully inverted, the model-Othello role falls back upon itself when the exile becomes the hired gun. In effect, he turns, or is turned, into a self- and ethno-traducing mercenary who withers, dangerously, in assimilationist illusions of distinterested merit and esteem.

It was out of such concerns with the exile as hired, or noble, gun, that character and voice developed into the second volume of the Sierra Leone trilogy, *Hand on the Navel*. The preoccupation explains why this volume's circumstances pivot as they do, around the years 1914-1918 and 1939-1945. After all, did not *The Sierra Leone Weekly News* (1884-1951), for one, take note on April 29, 1939, that Herr Hitler had remarked, and pointedly too, that "From time to time it is brought to notice that a Negro has become a lawyer, teacher, tenor or the like. This is a sin against all reason; it is criminal madness to train a born Semi-Ape to become a lawyer. It is a sin against the Eternal Creator to train Hottentots and Kaffirs to intellectual professions."

And in 1914, at the Feast of the Greater Biram, celebrated at Bonthe, Shebro, Sierra Leone, had not special prayers been "recited in solemn tones by Alpha Moukhtahr"—with two other Imams, Alimamy Duramany and Alpha Davendo, also officiating? For on the occasion of that Biram, after the recital of the ceremonial prayers, "a special form of prayers prepared for the present troubles of the war affecting Europe, the Empire and the civilised world were repeated." And the people there gathered had answered, "Amina." All the congregants had offered themselves up "on behalf of King George V, leader of his people, in the Kingdom and amongst the people whose capital is London. May God be merciful and hear our prayers, and the people say, Amina!" The Imam had led them further: "Grant that our armies be aided by angels and that they may have success and will speedily conquer their foe! Amina! The Kaiser is desirous to be dominant ruler over all, may he be unstable and fail in his purpose of tyranny. May God the merciful help the armies of the King and all who are concerned in the war on his side. Amina!" Appropriately, along with that November 14, 1914 Biram report, the *Sierra Leone Weekly News* had also carried the prediction of a certain Mme de Thebes, the celebrated French Prophetess, that "the Allies will win a crushing and total victory, and that the Kaiser will die a mental and physical wreck."

Granted, it was true enough that we were latitudes away from so "Yankee-boy" a thing as would happen on August

31st 1943, when a white private would tell a negro officer who had reprimanded him for not observing the ordinary military courtesy: "if you would take your clothes off and lay them on the ground I would salute them but I wouldn't salute anything that looks like you." For that was in another country; and as yet to be reported in the collection of letters from World War II "nigger-man" soldiers that Phillip McGuire would call *Taps for a Jim Crow Army* (1991). Such "taps" could hardly have been a live, and lived, thing with us.

Small wonder, that, ancient and loyal, the *SLWN* could reach out so to record, on November 7, 1914, the anxious agony of our exclusion: "'Oh, if the Government will only come to our aid and give us our desire. Talk of the coolness of the Turcos and the Senegalese as being cool under fire? Below the biggest zero will stand our coolness when we know we are on the path to meet the atrocious Kaiser and his infernal and barbarous host.' That's strong, isn't it? The sentiment, I am sure, will find an echo in every Creole boy's heart." For "the Creole boy loves the soldier life. He loves the smart uniform and the swaggery gait of the so'jer man. But he wants a chance to join the colours. Give him the hope of an epaulet, a star and a sword and, by Jingo! you'll see what stuff he is made of. How grand it would be, eh, if we could get a response called 'The King's Own Creole Boys'."

And in an October 7, 1939 appeal for "deeds not words," the *SLWN* would recall that there could have been no doubting the loyalty, "most gladly shown," of Sierra Leone. It must have been with due regard to the weight of authority that on September 3, 1939 His Excellency the colonial Governor General signed two orders "relating to the use of lights in Freetown"—on buildings with windows that faced the sea since, "for the present time," it was "not thought to be necessary to order that windows which do not face the sea should be covered." However,

> As from today no light shall be shown and householders are advised to take immediate steps to see that windows which face the sea are fixed in such a way so that no light, however dim, can penetrate, This is best done by fixing cardboard or several thicknesses of paper over the window.

Besides, this was all under circumstances in which it was not a matter to be taken lightly that His Majesty's Broadcast to the Empire had taken place on September 3, 1939. Moreover, on September 1, after it had been learned that Germany had invaded Poland, His Majesty had driven to No. 10 Downing Street for a talk with the Prime Minister Mr. Chamberlain. In 1941 he would again visit No. 10 to see, this time, Mr. Churchill, who had succeeded Mr. Chamberlain in May, 1940. Further, within a few years one of the largest sequestrations ever of the Empire's fleet of ships would take place in Freetown's well-positioned harbor. Such matters could not be forgotten, of course. And they would not be, neither in *Hand on the Navel* nor in *Highlife for Caliban*'s "The King of a Distant Country (1940-45)." For, pressed as "a memory at 78 rpm," it all came through in the wild and counterfeit passion of "baroque radios we did not invent." All in all, as that chronicle of record *The Sierra Leone Weekly News* put it in October of 1939, "it was deeply felt that we were part and parcel of the British Empire and that in England we lived and in England we died."

And it bears noting that this politics of passion and assimilation was certainly consistent with what an *SLWN* "Jottings" item had declared on November 21, 1914, at a time when "undoubtedly we [were also] concerned:" it never was an "over estimation of ourselves" to know that we were British subjects;" that we were "part and parcel of that conglomerate whole forming the population of the British Empire." And no statement to the contrary, "however trenchant, could eradicate from us the idea that the weal or woe of the British Throne or nation, has a more or less reactionary *(sic.)* influence on us." The "Jottings" columnist had been moved to respond thus because of a contrary opinion about our place in the imperial scheme of things. For it was his conviction that so contrary a view could not but be "merely a twaddle worked up to sincerity by prejudice (race prejudice) which generally reduces to temporary distortion the intellect of man." Besides which, another "Jottings" item noted, a donation to the British Red Cross war effort was "a positive indication that despite his ebony appearance, the Negro is in no way devoid of the spirit of humanity." And in this, "Jottings" was quoting a certain Dr. Awunor-Renner.

And, later, in such places as in *The History of Battalion of the Royal West African Frontier Force*, compiled by the likes of Lt. R.P.M. Davies from "the Official Records and Documents and from the Letters and Papers of Old Frontier Officers," it would be chronicled that Frontier Boys had indeed "been called upon to take part in a great struggle, the rights and wrongs of which they can scarcely have been expected dimly to perceive. They have been through the, to them, novel experience of facing an enemy with modern weapons, and led by highly trained officers. Their rations have been scanty, their bare-footed marches long and trying, and their fighting at times extremely arduous, yet they have not been found wanting either in discipline, devotion to their officers, or in personal courage."

In effect, what *Hand on the Navel* explores from and against the template of such matters is the model of Othello at war with himself and against his own, for Venice and Desdemona. But all this takes place in real time, and in real enough histories that have to do with Euro-America's and Japan's quarrels being transformed into two instances of global catastrophe. A quarrel and a catastrophe that were resonant, all the same, with Europe (and Othello) and Ottoman and Turk. For us, then, it was a resonance that could not but "take the biscuit"—as it certainly does when the *Sierra Leone Weekly News* chose to declare on November 14, 1914: "In the name of all that is sensible, what has possessed the 'sick man in Europe' to become entangled in the European imbroglio!...For consummate ingratitude Turkey, as John Bull would put it, 'takes the biscuit.'"

Shades in and of such matters account for the consequent, and true-to-life, dedication of *Hand on the Navel* to a soldier of the Royal West African Frontier Force (RWAFF), Sierra Leone Regiment:

> The book of Corporal Bundu, RWAFF, who came back insane; and all those others who apprenticed our youth to an enchantment of sorcery and madness; and teased magic out of the fire of strange women singing of blue birds over the white cliffs of Dover. This then is a recording of memories and half memories, of songs and half-songs—and of half lives.

There is a certain historicity in the finality to which these half lives come in *Hand on the Navel*—be it on the encrusted portuguese stone steps of the harbor in Freetown, or in Frankfurt and Marseilles; or else knee-deep in jungle-rot in Burma; or elsewhere, in Europe, where unmasked Senegalese soldiers coughed up their lungs under mustard gas attacks. Looked at in such ways, it turns out that sooner or later Othello will pretty much stab himself, or be stabbed, into a relevant if suicidal recognition of *how* he means in Venice. For the

RWAFF, the consequent reality was to be as much in plain chant as in dying to no good effect, and so far from "*the banks of old Moa River/where the moon shines so bright.*"

> *I leave my mother*
> *I leave my father*
> *I leave them farrr-rah-wayyy...*

> at Arnheim...
> in December
> we went
> slate-grey with cold
> and we left the corpses
> under a shred a moon
> and the dry wind cropped
> them into a white stone.
> the ground was a hard thing, sir...

And a recognition of sorts follows in the conclusion to which the RWAFF comes:

> to what end aim a dry root
> at italian carrara, thinking
> of villas and fine pissoirs?
> Mussolini died upside down.
> Rosa posed, but not for us,
> with a dulcimer. in Venice. You remember
> the picture. in Florence.
> what can a dry root do among them?
> in Venice the stones suck so at a green misery
> and sink so far now down from Ethiopia;
> and to what end? to have come
> this far with irregular steps, marching.
> to what doxologies does one pander
> now? Nijinsky danced and went mad.
> did you know? at the end.

"The mind of man is capable of anything," so Korzeniowski-Conrad's Marlow tells us. The observation is true, perhaps. But the confrontation with Difference, or to put the matter more gently, the exile from Sameness, that the man proposes with such flair and pithiness is no easy matter. Indeed, Marlow makes the observation shortly after the following disorienting confrontation between Self and Other:

It was unearthly, and the men were—No, they were not inhuman. Well, you know, that was the worst of it—this suspicion of their not being inhuman. It would come slowly to one. They howled and leaped, and spun, and made horrid faces; but what thrilled you was the thought of their human-ity—like yours —and the thought of your remote kinship with this wild and passionate uproar.

Here, the "passionate uproar" underscores starkly, even melodramatically, the ambivalent values that being foreign and being made to feel foreign can generate. It is note-worthy, of course, that the feeling originates in response to a somewhat stereotypical contact with "nigger" strangeness. This means that, even in its exile, "the mind of man" is already gifted with that familiar, pre-existing, condition of superiority (here "euro-white;" but also safari/tourist/national geographic/take-your-choice advantage).

Consider, in this light, the confusion of regression and refinement in which Guiseppi Verdi, Placido Domingo, and Othello meet, in a vignette from the 1993-94 New York Met-ropolitan Opera season. The passion and the uproar come, here, when Othello is deprived of vision. The social crisis and psychological scatteration that follow are ones which the "*Dio! me potevi scagliar tutti mali*" (Verdi/Arrigo Boito: act three, scene three) tries, and, hardly surprising this, fails to contain:

God! You could have rained upon me
all evil; all the misery, the afflictions
of shame; have made my trophies
and bold triumphs a ruin—a lie...
and I would have borne the cruelty of that cross
of anguish and shame; would have
resigned to the will of heaven;
and calm, borne it all.
But, oh the grief, the suffering!
they have deprived me of the vision
in which I joyfully kept a tranquil soul.
Dimmed is that sun, that smile
and the radiance with which it quickened me....
Clemency, you immortal power, once
a red-rose smile; cover up your sacred
face, now, in the hell-hot horror of rage.
    (my translation)

And when Placido Domingo gives voice to a pedigree for such anguish, the tenor of what he makes up is predictable enough: "At one point, Mr. Domingo changed the timbre of his voice," writes *The New York Times* critic Edward Rothstein in "Mr. Domingo Explains How He Does What He Does" (4/6/94), "making it seem pale, stripped of resonance or physicality. He does it again now, slowly gasping out the scarcely audible monotone Verdi wrote for the Moor. *'Dio—me potevi—scagliar*; it has the quality of a recitative,' he says, taking long breaths between phrases. 'I try to think of the almost guttural sound that this black man in a moment of desperation will have. He is a noble character,' Mr. Domingo continues, stepping back from the role, 'and he has been very much refined by the new culture, by the new religion, by the new people. What I like sometimes is when he feels deceit from everybody. He goes back to his roots, into his own world.'"

In the view that Placido Domingo thus represents, the confounding of identities is bound to be especially challenging—threatening even. For it is, signally, a matter of backsliding into roots. And it is in the face of what remains forever so guttural and irreducible that Marlow retreats, in the heart of his darkness, into an imperious assertion of Self as presence and plenitude. The "mind of man" thus summons to its rescue a set of non-negotiable first principles about what constitutes identity and value, and humanness. For the trick, says Marlow, is to breathe dead hippo meat, so to speak, and not be contaminated, because "I have a voice too, and for good or evil mine is the speech that cannot be silenced."

The exemplary meeting of human voice and hippo meat that Monsieur Theodore Monod provides us in *L'Hippopotame et le philosophe* (1941) is quite the appropriate one. And its appropriateness is nowhere more telling than when he leads us to an epiphanic moment in the life of Dr. Albert Schweitzer (missionary doctor to equatorial Africa; German-born in 1875 at Kaysenberg, Upper Alsace, now in France; groomed in philosophy and theology at Strasbourg, also in France, now). Schweitzer's epiphany is rooted in the heart of darkness; on the forested banks of the Ogowe river, no less. The moment comes when light plays against, and scatters, the dark: "*tout à coup, dans ces ténèbres va briller la lumière.*" And indeed it was so, even if Schweitzer's consequent management of insight and elbow-room was "somewhat patriarchal"—as the *Encyclopaedia Britannica*, fifteenth edition, gently notes. Still, there *was* light; and a great illumination it was. As may be noted from a recent American television synopsis of *The Light in the Jungle* (1991; starring Malcolm MacDowell and Susan Strasberg): "Dr. Albert Schweitzer and his wife face[d] a variety of hurdles while establishing a hospital in the jungles of Africa" (*The Ann Arbor News Television Guide*, August 21-27, 1994). "*Ecoutez le philosophe lui-même,*" Monod exhorts us. Which is what we get to do when Schweitzer recalls the signal translation from blindness to insight, on the third day: "*Au soir du troisième jour, précisément lorsque nous traversions un troupeau d'hippopotame, il me fut donné, tout soudainement, d'entrevoir la solution: respect de la vie. La porte de fer avait cédé. Je commençais à voir clair.*" In effect, where Newtonian physics had been, so to speak, "eureka'd" by the gravity of an apple's fall, for Schweitzerian insight into the decline and reconstruction of moral culture, into the import of Christianity and the religions of the world, for such insights to come there was hippo meat. Monod is succinct: "*C'est la pomme de Newton*" (337). No doubt, there remains much that is hippo-suggestive and irresistible about the continent. For in working out her 1980 "reappraisal in African history"—in early colonial eastern Zambia, this time—Gwyn Prins was moved to find epigraphic value and explanatory power for *The Hidden Hippopotamus* in the Luyana proverb, "The hippopotamus...swirls the deepest waters, the white sands of the shallows betray him."

Conditions of exile and insight in the last volume of the Sierra Leone trilogy, *Carnival of the Old Coast*, are set to work accordingly, in any number of refracting ways. These involve the volume's concerns with women, from Penelope knitting in Ithaca to the "long-nippled indigo women" of "Armistice," and the nine poems arranged into the sequence, "Hagar, or, The Insufficiency of Metaphor." The sequence draws from Judaeo-Christian narratives—and from the Islamic texture that the *Qur'an* and Al-Bukhari and Jalal-Ud-Din Rumi provide—for its treatment of exile and the temptation of allegiance:

how a slavewoman misunderstand
contract for fact of grace
jahweh too and miss sarah
— no less—is instructive;

        — so too
how a business can get
full so of wilderness and stone talk;
why it waits, still, to laugh
back, and rearrange.

Meanwhile, the poem "And regarding Penelope..." had duly called attention to the relevance of gender and sexuality in the politics of power and the privilege of choice. And it was in the conjunction of such issues that it found reasons enough why

the greek was luckier
regarding all this in himself.
busy, he could forget to think
how Ithaca sits
with her where she sits
to knit out the noise
of men sailing off to Troy,
and, below stairs,
a native clutter of sheep.

The poems of *Carnival* also place "the mind of man" and the "speech that cannot be silenced" in other ports of call: from the Dardanelles, "south of Istanbul," to "*Banzo*: A temptation of Brazil" (an inconsolable sadness that drove African slaves to various forms of suicide); and from the Manhattan of "The new year exiles" to the Argentina of "Witness" where

it hardly mattered that Buenos Aires would
lie, after the fact,
like an awkward sentence
on this reason or that word.

And throughout, such contexts are used to re-generate master texts and their attendant sub/versions; as happens when, in the Peru of the sixteenth century, Pizzaro pits himself against Atahuallpa. Up to a man's height in ransom gold, the Spaniard nonetheless leaves the Inka dead, to "grope in darkness":

a showerdust
in gold fell here, where the tribe,
   a light held to its heart,
looked to see if Self remained, or would
mirror some such thing in the dead reckoning of joy.

So, too, when in the Mexico of 1519 Cortes sets himself up against Moctezuma. As I interpret their meeting, what he offers the Aztec is the "consolation" of resurrection into a new identity. His promise, guarantee, even, to Tenochtitlan is, accordingly, that "the most miraculous roses will grow/ once again; take their root/in the choked residue of grief"— because

Whether this language
I speak hears only itself
out, and then is stranded
—*ad maiorem gloria dei*—

...
history has no embarassment
that endures higher than its rehearsal:
this bracing romp
that quickens us into worth.

Elsewhere—in the "Pedigree, with Weight" section of Carnival—"Corpse Cooking at Night" engages a history that appears to have no embarrassment. There being, after all, no such thing as an anthropology of (native) shame,

note, I am told,
the long firehardened wooden spear.
—and I do— Wooreddy holds it. others too.
their names cluster in consonants,
the vowels exuberant, drunk, weaving so:
"Maori Warrior Rings Bell at Whakariwarena"
"A Dinka in His Dancing Dress..."

note, I am told,
and I do so note, the dog.
in the foreground the dog
is a dingo, too...

with magnifying glass I go over
and over again the jawlines I see
nothing that I look at falls right
where the sunlight falls,
"Bantu Female, high arse, with deep face"
in the camera's shallow eye.

Still, my feeling is that it does some good to record refus-
als to surrender to the erasure of good sense and resilient
sensibility. Even when the mind of man sorely tempts us to
see nothing but "like to like, organizing chaos," there is, in
"the defiance of figures in wood," a carnival collection of
masks that we may yet get to wear, and to good effect. In
which case,

how could we sink?

the gods stand up for bastards:
in their own odd dance
they fall from the sky,
their foreskins peeled back.

we could kneel, too, on the sea,
ambitious as salt water
itself, and not sink; though the caked
hulls of ships, their ships,
when they depart, shake
the wakes we intend, or keep...

call us Ishmael (if you please) or Barabbas;
Habibatu or Zenobia. Cain, too.
we take a count in figure and in sum,
no matter how hissed as injury into the ear.
we barter coinage for coin, and do not sink.

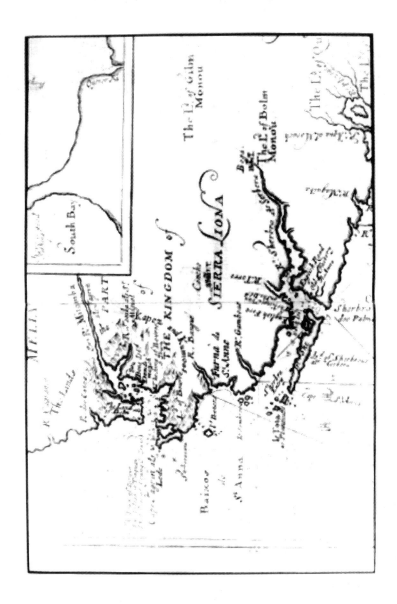

The Book of Corporal Bundu, RWAFF*
who came back insane

and all those others who apprenticed our youth to an enchantment of sorcery and madness; and teased magic out of the fire of strange women singing of blue birds over the white cliffs of Dover. This, then, is a recording of memories and half-memories, of songs and half-songs—and of half-lives.

*The Royal West African Frontier Force fought for the Allies in Europe, Africa, and Asia during the world wars. Corporal Bundu returned to walk the streets of Freetown, Sierra Leone, in all the spit and polish of his tattered soldiering.

They spoke of Abyssinia, Egypt, Palestine, Burma, and so on. Some of them had been village ne'er-do-wells, but now they were heroes. They had bags and bags of money, and the villagers sat at their feet to listen to their stories. One of them went regularly to a market in the neighbouring village and helped himself to whatever he liked. He went in full uniform, breaking the earth with his boots, and no one dared touch him. It was said that if you touched a soldier, Government would deal with you. Besides, soldiers were as strong as lions because of the injections they were given in the army.

Chinua Achebe, *No Longer at Ease*

PROLOGUE

*and with his swagger stick
and with his look-me-a-lady
and with the by the by that is
to come too, if you listen*

the pipes will call
down the mountain side
centaurs will trot down
to dance a dance of blood
in Flanders field,
        and you will
see such a sight!
a black man digging a long hole
in the middle of Europe
his bone-house broken.

with his swagger stick
and his by the by
yet to come,
        I tell you this:
you will sit by that beachhead
and devour the hot flesh of god;
and in that ecstasy of seeping blood
what will you do then
in that fecundation of dead
water and light?

...and what, besides,
after the fact of fire?
when they will have
said their *was willst du hier*
to you? and make of you
darkness impolitic come
to root in the body—
and taken so, in evidence;
        when at five
or less you believed that
woman, even that white

woman, had a penis
(*O Lorelei*, that it would matter so!)
hidden in Nuremberg or Bataan.

and "what, then, should I have called
myself? Bella Akhmadulina?
and so threaten Germany
with Petersburg and deep snow?

Marlene, my friend,
I remember, too, the height
of the guardhouse gate;
and the radio's black voice
in song, and me, going
to war, my name an embarassment.
and so short a name,
too, if you listen only."

we went skipping,
private no more, in brass
octaves and huptwos!
oga, we were marching
such a march.
I tell you with strong words
we were marching
a march: in hupfoot and down
foot and double quick
time such as we could
march, private no more,
and down into our very throat.

I leave   my mother
I leave   my father
I leave them farr-rah-wayy

such a song in defiance
of gravity and minor chords,
O king of England!
but who born you, eh?
when *we* are marching?

—when we are not
forming the fool;
and I swear it, bone to bone,
O King George, I leave
them all. and by ord'nance
and by arms! for wherever
march can be, we can march
and not pass this one.

we will not pass this cup;
and though the heart is not a bag
pipe, we can march to it.

O man Phillip,
and who, who, indeed, could
born you so to be
at the daughter's coronation!

when we were marching home
to Pretoria Pretoria Pretoria
        oh who could born you
to lie so and to come
where the frogs wait
in a pandering pose on lily pads,
the princesses denying all?

PART I

"O you whose eyes are painted, O girls
You and the rifle--what you command is done."

And what could we have known
of the pandemonium danced in his brain
in sure hope of promised resurrection;
when their feet, mother of god, were
luminous so over dark ways, (unruly so
in the urge to serve god with irrelevant children)
there, by the rotten waters of a dead river?

let me sit, then, at the feet of god and learn
"Moi, je fume, souvent ma pipe"—smartly—
I smoke often my pipe. and you will say
this trying to swallow your tongue
and the frenchman's congratulations,

medalled; but do you now know, he asks, what
a *krummhorn* is played on a rocky ledge? and what,
pray, of the beauties of all our persons,
one ear cocked so, eh? to the earth for
the tucket and boom of strange frequencies:

I can choose a girl to remember in Paris, France—
she was beautiful—"in a frisson
of the meat of crab and aquavit eaten!"
O you whose eyes are painted, O girls,
je fume souvent ma pipe, and learn, *moi*
myself that Ngoni litany, do you recall?

listen, you who are asleep,
who are left tightly closed in the land
shall we all sink into the earth?
listen, O earth, the sun is setting tightly,
we shall all enter into the earth.

w'rant of'cer of the day! to have suffered
such a change on their ships

for the medalled kisses of a frenchman,
when the limits of these worlds are stone,
and grave, too, beyond the drift of water and weed,
or ships those englishmen called dreadnaughts.

II

and here? with us now where death still
distributes his gifts one by one,
though the heart is not a bag
into which one merely plunges the hand?
stone wears down a man's patience
with simpering imbecilities; and ground
out in slow bits, the stumps of our lives
wait to be shovelled out of cold ovens.

you could stumble over skulls, he says
he knows this, rising, so he says,
to the imperative of such music;
you could grow old too, with the girls—
you know, the girls—decrepit then in their skin
petticoats, and near enough to bone, saying,
one cannot help a man so unlucky,
the girls denying all, you know—

"though I offer this my heart on a tin plate,
in this my left hand is a glaucous eye
for the rascalities, I tell you, of women
not made to be sucked!"—for the mouth comes
to then, bone-filled and broken, O Bundu.

PART II

III

For now

I take great satisfaction
reading the obituary notices:
the war goes badly, *memsahib.*

IV

it was, after all, in a far-off place he died
and came back with a bony left hand.
he died and came without elegance of proof,
his face quick, still, with metaphor:

        that was the summer,
        in the antics of
his odd corners, he kept the eye
of a ravaged penis tight
in his left hand.

        a strange summer.
drywhite.
for vivid waitings. the earth
cracked in thirst. and the dry holes
of those women portable so with sin!

        a strange summer
and the woman saying, he says,
he was nonsense, "contumelius nonsense"
and he saying: "the intellect is god's fire"

for when Napoleon invaded Egypt
avec la loh-ray-nay et avec mes sah-boh
it was not oo lah a thing at all ordinary

O dealer in levitation,
O white *soldati* in song

and debauched, he sings,
now in the very throat of hell,
the night is no more
than a mocker of tact:

for what do you think now? will she come
now to this your bony left hand
to die in a delicious lasciviousness?

V

there are no rabbits in Malaya,
                              sir.
there was one who knew that, saying
so. (despite the nets, the
mosquitoes insistent); and quinine is
as bitter as death is not sweet.

what then did they die for? their boots
militant on stone,
                              there
was a captain gave orders then
that each man catch twenty five
flies, presenting arms on parade;

to build latrines is one answer,
shore down the bowels, ease
the stiff seduction of grist in whistle and march:
cpl. Bundu, Sierra Leone Royal Volunteer, mad
so for triumph, too, in that other film
that he alone could see:

VI

it was to a musicale he went—and came
feeling so to us, out of place (and
we came, a suicide note, too; dead-
ly dull), with black lace fringing
the mouth (and there sucked
the trumpet and the reveille, off-key)

with the taps full of deft diapasons
a deft concord of notes, and the ships
fullbodied, riding stops in the harbor

VII

becalmed,
educing landfall against the flumes
of white water, De Ruyter (believing in
the catalytic fact of admiral and stone) left,
for *canzone*, a stone in Sierra Leone.
it squats there, in the bay;

a sour stone that,
educing temptation and strange truth
(inciting indifference before the Atlantic):
"You cannot cure the pox
with yet further whoring"
for, then, water thickens.

VIII

but what if
the daughter of a british civil servant
should sing (to him) from a high verandah,
and he, in red, shuddering in release,
and would lie so in her water...

and if he should lie in her water
and if he should lie so in the king's own
waters, and there become a growth of coral?

what then?

he had thought it continent and possible;
perforce, he would coerce
and stroke the motions of war
into a head redolent of delinquent rituals.

and what then?

IX

she had the smell, *mmobrowa*,
of a woman not yet awakened--
to limit the gain

X

O, yes, lord, she had, man,
the smell of a woman not yet awakened
bringing thoughts of fish, gutted
live in the waters, slippery—
full so of the bayonet unsheathed—
blind in the eye and wet;

sweetly eccentric, and undeft, the blood flows
now into the ridges of the palm
from the suicide attempt; wherever
it is that thought follows flesh,
on parade, private
and peacock so in himself no more.

XI

in nineteen thirty six, circa,
I think, he says, there was a landslide; the earth
tired; red-ridged, those huge boulders fled
down the soil at Charlotte,* inescapable
their roots in nuggets of black-tumored stone.
you see them in the gorge; behind the bay;
wherever it is, the memory follows you;

*Charlotte, a village, like Regent and Bathurst, but the
furthest in and above the Freetown peninsula.

XII

and wherever it winds, the road leads
(for a man cannot be separated from his acts)
past the dirt of granite and shale:
where his father lies, *farr-rah-way*, he says,
and buried, in ventilated cokestones
("my father is a dead man;
I have left those cokestones
there, lacking carrara and epigraph")

XIII

and for this
he sat that summer on portuguese steps, limned
in stale iron, on edge
and spat through
the front holes of his teeth.

and for this,
in a dirty blouse,
she bends again for him at a table.
she, for a metier,
stepping down (the waters green with
salt over those portuguese steps)
and he again ready to burst her undergarments.

such eating.

XIV

(in spite of temptations deep water is dark)
you remember how it was, he says,
the bugler's mouth gnawed to teeth
by brass. and only the dead

smiling, pulling back the mouth
under a mound of earth. you hear
the eager root reach for a face

heavy and liquid with rot,
the bugler's mouth, full, in key

and he after such eating.

XV

who then would not say
he was most reasonable
to be, and for such as he,
excited of Leni Riefenstahl,
and that other one too, who could
tap the *Blue Angel*, even,
and white-thighed,
lean back so to be
fringed in black lace?

*oh, these women, such women
as these*, will be ours
        to hold on, yet; stiff
with presenting and arms, ours
to meet and to meet again
for quick remembrances,
till these blue skies
drive the dark clouds away.

            (and pushed deep
into France, in his tourniquet
and his morphine; in his sleep
at a gate not easy to come by
we will create a world for two
—in ourselves private no more
than is a concrete pool, a small garden
of abbey and stone; this our memory
of hedgerows that knocks so at the heart)

and in Sicily and Africa,
*these women, such women
as these*, O Lili Marlene,
they will give me a rose

too, and Mandalay; they will
tie to the stem
love, only, that renews itself.

and who else would say it,
then, if not himself, that
it was reasonable (for him)
to march *hupfoot* and down
and *hupfoot*, his boots,
each one, a different color
where the purple lily, alone, will grow,
raising the dead, the fine hard dead.

for so he came, cpl. Bundu,
                    becalmed.

XVI

here, at the corner of the world
I eat these my remembrances, and suck
this and other testimonies of the misbegotten
from my fingers to the second joints.

and the eyes of the dead dancing,
and they alone thinking it the end of war.

and here, besides, where it was beauty of form,
once, that white-frocked girls
would raise the thigh, raise the inside
so of the thigh, to walk in their yellow shoes.

PART III

XVII

but for the canonical testaments of the idle,
at highwater numbers have no synonyms,
the tales undeceive at highwater:

we had come, he could think it, to find
out how it was his boots were danced
so to pieces; doing him (cantankerous sorcerer!) damage.

XVIII

but it was great, ah, it was great,
and daring-brave, to be young
then. and we were all happy
together. at the same time.

       (and the needles
pointed, and coppery inside
the gramophone, to the last degree
and dance profligate,
daring the furtive opening of thighs;
and the tailbone tight-hard
in thrust, held no longer at bay)

XIX

to think so, now
that the flies eat out the dissonant
arpeggios of our meat, a whole
regiment of sons, memsahib.

it was a hard thing, sir,
(the daring preamble of flesh
cross-hairing the intimate bone)
to think it so now.

XX

there was once a widowed king,
*tantang jali**, red in his red mahogany
girth, *tantang jali*, once upon a time,
and deep with his waters and his boots,

and with them his "daughters,
his, maiden, daughters of a widowed king,"
coppery of flesh, inlaid
so, and still. then to be torn to shreds,
wherever it was noblemen could
pluck so and pick so at women such as these.

and even on such poppy days—we all
the while were marching—we were
marching home to Pretoria Pretoria,
we were marching home so to Pretoria
with the princesses, and they denying
all; and King George dying late
and royal in his red mahogany girth
with his rivers and his boots

(and we who had marched off
peaked and plucked so
in hauerberk and pike;
we who came back, and went marching,
we did not live well thereafter)

and what then?

*jali, (sahelian West Africa; the Gambia)—thus, also *djeli* or *griot,*
or *belen tigui* (Master of the Tree Trunk in the Public Square).
He may be, say, lower-level *danno* (hunter's) or *mansa* (court)
keeper/singer of the archives. As a rule, he played the *kora*, a
twenty-six string harp-lute, with flamenco-guitar virtuosity. (The
danno kora is smaller, a six-string *simbingo*).

XXI

you remember now
the arabian sea keeping to itself
in narrow creeks,
and the small lamps flickering,
Bakhia Nairan undone,
pale with the imperfections of small cruelties,
and among the windings of that
unmade sea you remember
the tapping telegraph:

"Eritrea undone,
                    DUCE, undone.
salvare il salvabile"

and the coastline behind us
and the ethiopians skittish with spears
and the italians luminous with intent
and we, like the arabian sea, keeping faraway—

and with the "*soldati bianchi e salvabile*, do
you read us, do
Mussolini DUCE
DELLA PROVVIDENZIA, do you read this now?"

—and so faraway, too.

XXII

once, there were tales, *tantang jali*,
we knew so long ago, ending
then in a terrible rage:
mountain goats do not get friendly
with wolves; rats do not marry cats;
the bull strokes
into stone the beautiful maiden
heart—where he thinks
to seek a permanent residence

but, I tell you,
it was great, eh,
it was great
to be young; and raging
so were the things
then to be young
for—and be brought to attention—
seeing as how we were not yet stillborn.

XXIII

could I, then, have sung
myself into a note
as in a pavane for dead sorcerers, seeing
then that I would have no wife to comb
out her hair by a high window?

and could I ever know to sing
the harsh cough of frightened men,
for the black rot of all the young men
bent low on poppy and field?

XXIV

we came across the face
of a white man dead and,

his death too flippant,
we pried open his mouth
for with his tongue
we would coin a high joy.

(but, first of firsts, to have been
pusillanimous so,
and combed by lust at milady's high window!)

a meticulous gentleman it was
in the small appetite of flies,

the hair a stark provocation
on the stinking rot of a bone.

we came across the face
of a white man dead,

beguiling a rainy season
by the arabian sea,

where the earth is a trenchant must,
a banked bed of a skeletal sort.

XXV

here, in the wash of stone steps and bay,
you remember the clangorous passion of tanks
the profane prancing of many tanks,
the broken jawbones hungry with teeth
on a quiet front.
            and, *oga,*
for all that laugh can do only is laugh—

they say the houses of Molu in Tomboke are fine
that the houses of Molu are fine
the houses of the redstone cliffs

—and all of this and more, he says, is to laugh
more than laugh can remember alone as laugh.

XXVI

it was in the radio we first grew up
in a childhood we now see
made tinny with the nostalgia
of when white women were in song;
when there was some talk, besides,
of Alexander and some of Grenadiers,
and tro-ro-ro ro-ro-ro;

and with but a little more of
oh *rule! rule, yet, britannia,*
and with trumpet and bugle and *ro-ro-ro...*

for all the world's heroes made
up and high, for all and for them, too,
this love that was new, O Lili Marlene,
(black lace beyond
the barracks fence, and the round
round meat of a breast);
                    dizzy so to be
higher than is the height of a guardhouse
gate where we listened and grew,
growing mad with a counterfeit passion.

PART IV

XXVII

it cannot be profitable to abide a post
unadorned; or just to have killed a corpse.

we could leave now, and go to Córdoba
and there shake banners for a dead bullfighter;
indelicate, we could dance a polonaise
for bull and for Guernica besides;
and for Federico Francisco against the wall
shake a castanet of quick bones
in the beat of the slow drum in spain,
where an old woman in her black shawl
bends to better note the indifference of white stone.

        but at Verdun
this dead drift of meaning is ordinary,
still: the world is a private place
there, and harbors impenitent loyalties.

XXVIII

this Corsica is a granite island, sir.
its stones will come down on us, and for nothing, sir.
here, where, effendi-sir, we are the inferiors of inferior
devils.

but, my god! adorned, I could play the swashbuckler
even so, were not the hanging sword red
now, and beyond the rust of romance and emperor.

        still, the note holds
a deft thing in its temptation:
I walk with the crushed swash and buckle
that is Rosa or Bianca, or Josephine;
do you get the drift?

"A gentleman does not whip an innkeeper
because he doesn't like the wine, merely"

dressed, his remark and the note mount so
with us to where I plead myself a believer
in metempsychosis; and am disposed to
a sequence that is fair, with tempered blade

(I would pose this milady, and *en garde* make her
plead so for a good man
gone in, and to her high high window)

but sir, there is no profit in abiding
unadorned; to remain
where the killing of a corpse, sir,
is ordinary, and just to the point.

this Corsica, sir, is ordinary:
a granite island that calls to attention
the holes where we blink and stare with stones.

XXIX

I could repeat this and, more than this,
he says, the tattered incubi of names:
a memory of comical dogs
marching—*by the right,*
and about face, too,
under a shred of moon--

down to where we came in the hot mouth
of that creek, by the left,
in the tattered anthems of some native adulation;

and where a body could eat a woman's,
whole, we came then to the warm breast
and body, and we called for it to be
a hanging silliness, having learned;
and all for a dare, besides.

XXX

I remember a straight line of men
at Arnheim:
>   (style hardens into life
>   and you may, if you wish,
>   sir, dance on my coffin;
>   the boards are strong
>   and will tease magic out
>   of this line of fire)

in december
we went
slate-grey with cold
and we left the corpses
under a shred of moon
and the dry wind cropped
them into a white stone.
the ground was a hard thing, sir,
>   unkind.

XXXI

and you you and you, come too
soon to attention,
>   and, *oga*, you!
who born you so in quick
march and who born you
in double quick time
and, *by the right*, to slow march so?

drill corp'ral of the day,
O baboo-bone,
drum-sergeant and sergeant
major, swing the arm,
with a *hupfoot and right
foot*, and a sharp
smart wheel to the left,
of'cer of the day,
with a sharp right too,

and a left smart
enough to make the wind obey

and you, mister ability, you,
and mister you! who born you
to be a husband for ellua!
who born you,
mister blocos man,
to be husband for esi ellua,
O warrant of'cer of the day!
we give full marks for smartness
and these our small stones that hiss
up so to heaven
and by the left, *yeh*
and by the right, *yeh*

well, we na london boy,
yeh, we na london boy,
first class and ready to go
but s'c'n class we go
Cameroon* war, soja!

XXXII

for there once was a close and dry
knocking of stone against stone
                    (this we heard too)
f*or there'll always be an England!*
and England shall be free;
if only England means as much
to you as me. so, do nothing,
oh, do nothing till you hear from me.

"and do nothing at all, besides, till you hear,
from me in the beauty of all my person!"

*The Germans held trust territories in Africa, among them Togo
  and Cameroon, down the West African coast from Sierra Leone.

and here, where a jagged tin can can
meet the booted foot, and set the white
bone on edge; and with all the unquiet
dead at Lidice* to come, and their graves
moving, he said; like fields of corn,

he said, "when the devil takes the peacock's
beauty so into his mouth, do nothing,
oh, do nothing till you hear from me,
marching, in the beauty of all my person."

XXXIII

for this our march
will be a thing
of spit and a thing of polish
for marching; for what we are
is march. and we will march
this one down to Mandalay
            and march itself:
for hupfoot, *yeh*; and
for downfoot, *yeh*; for this one
too, and the king's own self
shogbor   eewor

I *leave   my mother*
I *leave   my father*
I *leave them farrr-rah-wayyy*
you who hear this, and under
your shred of moon are adrift
on the banks of old Mo-a ree-vah
drill corp'ral of day,
and you, w'rant of'cer
oh, w'rant of'cer,

*On June 10, 1942, German troops would erase the village of
  Lidice (Central Bohemia); all the men were shot; the women
  sent to a concentration camp; the children dispersed.

make this our gravel
and the granite
shake like *shegureh**
in a crack-dry skull
beyond even Swedru;*

and hiss them up to the ear
of god the father
and the ear of god the son
for who born you after all?
for who after all can born we
to attention such as this?

XXXIV

"once, their children, *tantang jali,*
were birds and stones

and the stones became men
and the birds became women."

and in the misturns
and turns of attention
there are old photographs
of people in high gladstone collars.

"and ever since they say
nothing but *gah-rah-gah;*
though, once, it was
the hero's duty (at the end)
to be born to marry a princess.
for who would preach heresy then,
or think the new songs possible?"

*music gourd, with cowrie shells; *"Yes, there is a man near
Swedru who is renowned for his juju to make you immune to
gunshot" (K.A. Bediako, *A Husband for Esi Ellua*).

XXXV

"Kitchibiria," (and *this* we did not ask)
"who born you so, Kitchibiria,
to drink blood from a throat

where a hard river will crumble;
where all that shoot can do is shoot?"

slapped now by poltergeist and war
in Mandalay and Flanders field
we are not new, as we were before—

english-flecked that we are!
and cropped to the very root
to find it a good thing
so to be: we—kakodaimon now
and autographed—in the enthusiasm for death;

and *what manner of man
is this*, then, what manner,
eh, to be marching so to Jerusalem
with all and fire in his eyes?

when all that the dead can
be is quietness; and you, alone,
left to remember how it was
to be when the bugler's
mouth is gnawed to teeth
and by brass; or the dead faces
that smile; how they pull back the mouth

to be under a mound of earth
and make the eager root reach
for a face liquid with rot,
and the full bugler's mouth in key.

XXXVI

do you call us now to such eating?
and Mizushima, too? frontispiece
for seasons of high mystery
we are yet to know
at the feet of a fat stone god,
clear, in the Chindwin river?

and for *hanyu no yado* when it is
all the same? and Mizushima is
to be him? and all of himself,
on a Burmese harp,
then, and longing so for home?

*The Chindwin is the main tributary of the Irrawaddy river, in
Burma—as is Mandalay, incidentally. *"We had always thought
Hanyu no Yado was a Japanese song, but it is actually an old
English melody [*Home Sweet Home*]...Whenever they hear it,
they think of their childhood, of their mothers, of the places
where they grew up. And so they were astonished and moved
to hear...the dangerous enemy they had surrounded in the high
mountains of Burma singing this song." (Michio Takeyama, *Harp
of Burma*).

PART V

XXXVII

and when you have after all
this cursed and damned yourself,
(and have gone too far and shot a white man
yourself with a gun) good lord let
the latin priest come then
with his fine ululantems, with
his sempeternal ululantems
for all the faithful now on their way;

and when after all this you stay to wrestle
with women, and keep the fingers close
in the quick of their
breasts where the nipples rise
to taste of salt and sweat,

then, let the latin priest come
with his ululantems, too; and think you
in the ecstasy of a fine crucifixion.

but yourself think of slaughter
and hot entrails; of the sempeternal riot
and rot of hot entrails—*radex malorum*,

indeed, for the root of all evil is there
in the devil's claws; where you keep a finger cocked
on hot breasts, remembering a fat
god who sits, for all you know, still
sits, open-thighed by the Chindwin river.

your knees like iron on parade,
or are flexed, only to stand at ease: you who had thought
it possible to go dancing all the while,
and no matter, in yourself, in Berlin or in Burma.

XXXVIII

"from a height of waterspouts and gargoyles
the bullets came skipping in high octaves
where there was, *effendi*, no last judgement,
only choice pieces of the heart.

the quick sopranos came singing
their tart intent;
                    I saw them
in the long procession of their lines.

and may god the father damn
our arse, lieutena' of the day, but
I saw them in their long procession."

and he would talk of the meticulous
craft of pillbox and hats, of Irrawaddy.
of passionate women,
                    later, it would be
that a *madamasel* lay open-legged
against a strong wall in the very heart of Europe.

XXXIX

"*madamasel*, keep us in mind," was where he had
it started, when we stayed to be caught
in his chant and dance of a small sorcerer:

"but may god the father damn their arse
but may god the son damn their arse
but may god the holy ghost damn their arse
and quick quick
and let the latin priest go stiff
too, let him go;
for who the fucking hell born them all, after all?"

XL

now, once upon a time,
men more wicked than Hitler
put *madamasel* on a wall
and look, man, how she can't *do the fuck-all*
at all no more, is what we think to hear him say.

(once upon a time,
he had come back with a cut stone
from under a cathedral,
on it was a He-Goat rode a woman
to tempt the appetite so!
the rough forelegs and the cloven hooves
erect with a stiff passion).

and his talk was a tart
thing, and a hot fire
with us, who found
it no disrelish,
then, to look so upon a looking glass.

XLI

become a deadweight, the heart
aches so against the dry skin.
and the pregnant mountainside does
too, but will open no longer
at the invocation of a mere word.

a man will die for standing
for too long at attention,
when the long years
do not save us from barbarisms.

whether or not adorned,
you lift stoppers from scented flagons
to find what they most serve
here deadens the brain, leaves the teeth
naked and on edge.

and the dry skin aches
for alchemy, for the sublimation
to come in dead stone.

XLII

once upon a time,
a small finger curves outward
from fine tea in a porcelain teacup;
the saucer lies, herb-scented.

(perhaps the bloodstained earth loves us a little?)
the heart beats with blood,
and you remember now that
you put an arm around the graceless
bones of a small waist,

the radio saying so,
in the king, my lord's chamber.
outside, the tongues of grass
stiffen into thin-sharp whispers:

"only a great stone holds down
the underthings of a woman drowned
in this the king's red river,
tomorrow, just you wait and see—"
the radio's voice saying so,
—until we meet again, he says, and set
to leave; we think he is set to leave.

we'll meet again, for he knows this
much about some sunny day, when, perhaps,
the bloodstained earth will move to love
us a little more than it is possible to be loved.

XLIII

(look! these pointless bones I rattle here
were once meat cooked, did you know, in an oven
in a Rhineland forest)

and you, you, you, and you
would you then have maimed
yourself not to serve?
              would you, as you think
now, have maimed yourself? so
as not to serve—and become yourself
your own swollen scrotum, fit only
to be carried about in a wheelbarrow?

(that pink-rich throat in the full
anguish of song over the white cliffs of Dover,
would you have maimed yourself not to serve
for four and twenty blackbirds,
for four and twenty virgins,
young, and come, besides, from Inverness?)

XLIV

timmini yimre
for so the song is sung, *tantang jali,*
to us here, where you wipe your hand
on the navel with us to talk
of a relationship that itself
is deeper than enmity:

a fly crossing the sky holds no meaning
nor the small skulls that mark some
imprecise horizon in the middle of Europe;

not now that you speak in a low voice,
your fingers in earnest over your lips:
"too many things roam through our nights;
the statue of Cecil Rhodes, for example,
standing in the middle."

and what is our nugget of fact,
we think to ask, in queen victoria days?
what else, but two englishmen shaking hands

in their presumption of
a dead continent?
the bearers cropheaded and silent,

and we, what else were we but
"black so as hell, and thick as grass"*
in queen victoria time,
when two ewes and a ram could guard
the corners of paradise, and fail;

and in a potful of blood
the lake unnamed would wait
to be named victoria.

XLV

but the landscape, to come, is not austere
with us: for what of Circe, with illustrations?
for she, *of all the girls, she*
alone is darling so
of my heart, and lives in our alley:

an anxiety of hurdy gurdies
and musical boxes looks to find
the seam in our aching brain:
and happy days are soon come (again)
and, man oh man, there come
a tavern in the town, you know?

in queen victoria day
good lord tell me
she get rings on her fingers
and fine bells on her toes;
see, once, how the lady ride a cock
horse too—and we are not ever
again the owner of our days
in queen victoria time!

*this, the word at the Battle of Rorke's Drift, January 22, 1879—
when, it being *ngatha mpi* (time for war), the Zulu Army of
Heaven faced, and lost to, a band of English soldiers.

the queen my lady is after turning
sunlight to moonlight
in queen victoria time, and *Tom Pierce,*

*Tom Pierce, oh lend me that gray mare
all along, down along, up along;* for, hupfoot so,

look now how the lady keeps
her breasts, full and fair
ones alike (*cherries ripe,
oh cherries ripe*) shaped,
like a long ewer,
and ripe so, I cry, coming
down to buy, and ready more
than money itself can hope to be ready.

well, then, I ask you
in a tavern in this town:
man, when she and all take their leave,
did we think to laugh behind our sleeve?

XLVI

and for four and twenty blackbirds?
and for four and twenty virgins from Inverness?
would you, then, in sure
and promised hope of resurrection,
oh, would you have maimed
yourself, not to serve?

besides, what price the statue of a victorian man
in the middle of a continent? such knowledge.

XLVII

it does little good to threaten us
in high marble!
              but in nineteen twelve
you remember a ship going down
in disregard of icebergs—and,

nearer then my god to thee,
such knowledge! my mother weeping
for fine people gone to water.
legends of a childhood, I ask you!

fete and bacchanal are
and nearer to god, you say.
in a people's carnival
can it be rickets alone that keeps
a man's legs bowed, and his groin
in fever and pitch?

in 'fifty-three they coronate a queen `Bet'
and who the devil going to stop that carnival?
you just bound to jump up and shake the brain bone
in a hot damn carnival

in 'fifty-three they coronate a lady
in a coronation, and you, shuddering
so in red uniform and delegation!
(O Phillip! man among men!)

and in a westminster chamber—well, I ask you!
how you manage, brother,
to climb Jacob's ladder so, and serve?

XLVIII

how you manage to serve and reach
such knowledge, when, with his one vowel
you have heard a Qawashgar Indian sing
himself into a still photograph, grained with age?

(oh, let them kill the Qawashgar Indian?
that, too, is a need, perhaps?)

but you would have us
keep to yourself now; and leave
the Magellan Strait to go
where it goes toward penguin and snow?

"the universe is unsatisfactory
enough, and seeks the face of a knight,
but toxic so with armor and quick thrust."

you think it enough that the straits
go where they go, to penguin and snow.

XLIX

and to what end aim a dry root
at italian carrara (he says), thinking
of villas and fine pissoirs?
Mussolini died upside down.
and Rosa did not pose for us,
with a dulcimer. in Venice. You remember
the picture. in Florence.
what can a dry root do among them?
in Venice the stones suck so at a green misery
and sink so far now down from Ethiopia
and to what end? to have come
this far with irregular steps, marching,
to what doxologies does one pander
now? Nijinsky danced and went mad,
did you know? at the end.

L

and whatever shall I do back in Frankfurt,
now? visiting Frankfurt, a superior guest
at a prussian wedding of coyly-turned anecdotes:
"do you remember the senegalese soldiers
flamboyant in cape and gas? do you?"
and when they ask *warum sagen sie "fromage"*?
they'll have us by the edge of the trousers!
and embarrassed so into another age,
and shaking a foreleg—we are embarrassed as
not even a dog can be embarrassed.
(and Spengler, toxic with melancholia!)

"I shall go about their cobbled walks—
this much; and let the girls ask *was willst?*
in the film where they will say,
it never was bullets that killed the beast.
was willst du, then?" or was it beauty,
like a deadweight, and shored up
against tomorrow, just you wait and see?

LI

we have returned too
to France. there is a cathedral
there in Marseilles, flaked in gold,
where the dead drift of the sea waits below.
I remember the stone steps.

I would go on living, for a change
there, even with an iron cross on my khaki.
I am not one to be like Flaubert
my every line the coffin of a dead illusion.

LII

I would live, have the girls come.
in the cantinas I hear them eat roses.
in their time, and in the quicksteps of blood,

they will teach me Argentina and tango;
tell me secrets of the timber
supply of ancient Rome. of Greece, perhaps.
(musical bones and gentle succubi,
such knowledge, may yet come to be)

LIII Armistice

and, *memsahib*, all the black born dead,
they may yet in their turn, dance, too;
thank woman and virgin for darkness,
lifted and to come; if they cannot do so

for the red canna lilies of Burma, unregainable
now among the small roofs of some god's alien pagoda;

and I may yet revert to myself in these late
afternoon tilts of the head—remain, posed
just so, like a cockatoo cresting in mid-equator.

(so, shut the blood's gate.
I have seen the sign on a fence:
this is the land of dogs and flies.
shut the blood's gate. keep
at least the dogs out)

and it will be some other river (beyond
what time I have) that foams on
its way with dying bone and green entrail.

Vademecum

REQUIEM FOR A LAPSED CATHOLIC
(*vademecum* for carty caribbean)

introit

what good comes of it
when we stand, naked,
flesh to flesh,
but in the bite
of an eccentric tooth?

inferno

in their dreams
let them laugh
at the yellow yolk
they think is your eyeball;
but god give you
attention and catechism,
O Carty Caribbean, even
in their dreams of you:
all of them, the sons of god
shouting, and for joy,
in their yellow dreaming
of you, a body agape,
and ready (*ora pro nobis*!)
to open the flesh-
filled trunk like
a knot-hole, ambitious
as only a cheap
cunt can be ambitious
in these their dreams
of you, and fingered
so against the disregarding
flame-tree and star-apple

purgatorio

but could we,
oh, would we
have sailed up so,
            instead,
in a cannibal river
where the long
gorillas mate
once a year?

what ark would hold
back the deluge
of the life to come then?

and what will we do
in promised mansions
winged to Miss Rose
and bent so
for Master Horn,
too,
under a slow-turning
and tropical fan?

and if it turns out
what you eat, if
the joy of it
all, it turns out, fails
on the tongue,
under a bighouse verandah,
what then?

in paradisum

but how the mouth can
sing so to work
in over-praised seasons!

when we are no more
bent to eat ashes

when we are no more in
the touch and the trouble
of lent in a tight mouth!

blessed be
the dead then,
upon whom the rain
will fall no more.

in that season,
instead, of high hosanna
and holy water
deus amet et puellam
et intactam,
let god love
this our girl.

o carty caribbean,
lady and intact
at last, deus amet te.

POSTMORTEM FOR A RESURRECTIONIST

adam in the presence.
himself, too, in the garden.
adam was in the presence of god
yet he hid himself in the garden.

So, Peter, go ring da bell!
and with power more than god conceive
to fit in muscle and locomotion,
call all the water of the world;
Peter, you go ring da bell!

for enormous with thrust, the sea
king's daughter will arise
then. ah telling you, man, call
so she rise to come in a sea shell,
the sea king's daughter, rising
to make temptation come so,
and in a sea-shell, too.

and the purple-red lips
the purple mouths of the dead
go tipple over our fence
then; and catch the throat
from under the odd stone;
go fill our heads, empty now,
with the must that is
the graveclothes smell
of each man putting up
his old kit bag; his own
self's day drawing close to be,
nearer my god to thee, like shadows
of the evening, marching as to war.

COMPLINE
(Finney Chapel, Oberlin)

mother of god, *regina coeli*!
if she had an inch more thigh
you could dance a tarantella
to make the grass bloom
and all the world's houses
vanish down in one verdict

itself, *mater dei*, alone
and yes and us together
if she had an inch more
thigh to show! now and in the hour.

11

these high presumptions of beams,
and you, all the while
in a tantrum of petticoats:
now and in the hour.
et semper. full so of grace.

*compline: the seventh and last of the canonical hours; also, an
attendant night song, as here, to *regina coeli*, queen of heaven.

CARIBBEAN SUGAR
(Matilda's corner, Kingston)

> *I have already mentioned that a certain Avilon*
> *de la Vega was the first man to make sugar in Cuba.*
>   -Padre Bartolomé de las Casas

The first time, then:
whatever else it was
the traffic could bear,
the need was great.

and deadcrazy too when she
look so to make a body's brown,
or white, self intact,
again, in all its parts

(like sweetness in a tight place,
and under the naked leg
of a man deaddrunk in his heart

for nightfall); when she bends
down and stirs, and make corner
and corner meet like canebrakes
that rise to a strange clamor of joy.

till you come; till you think:
too far west is when you reach
east, and make paradise rise
then like sudden ecstasy can
make rightfoot even of a lefthand place.

SWAGGER STICKS

swagger stick:
a short light stick typically capped at both ends with metal
or covered with leather and intended for carrying
in the hand (as by military officers)

CONVERSION OF THE ETHIOPIAN EUNUCH

was a weddin' in Canaan
haile selassie an' 'im mudder was there
dry bones come outa de valley

lean heavily on the spectacular
then, before the gods reach down
to kick you in such high love;

II

and think now of Leda compliant,
under a bird's conversion.
nothing happens quite by accident;
the aim was Troy. shattering the gates.

III

these somnambulant places
too many times fingered:
how does one get through
the rest of our lives—
even if the earth does
revolve, really, around the sun?

IV

in these the last cool days:
hyde park in the afternoon,
tea time at trafalgar
among the flight of pigeons is all.

SHORT VISIT TO AUSCHWITZ

He set it up in the plain of Dura,
province of Babylon.
Book of Daniel, *2; 1.*

Push hard enough:
and the lines converge
beyond province and the plain
temptation of screen and stage.

you recall, though, three men,
jews, urgent, dancing in a fire.

and, if you wish, say it:
that all this was play,
      a long time ago;
that the earth was young
then, full too of blank
spaces in the heart.
      and three jews,
dancing in their time,
god-crazy so in their coats,
their hose and their hats?

for all that, the king sits
to look, golden on his throne;
he thinks to make this thing
a scene that is,
      and is to be,
a triumph in his will,
superb so in flames of fire.

A CELEBRATION IN ISTANBUL

no man alive today can know which
side's dead mean will win the war

But I should have been here then.
south of Istanbul, I mean; squeezer

of concertinas for Cassandra the mad
knowing now in a book of numbers of other

men's dead men inside the belly
of the greek's horse, waiting. to have been

alive and to know the secret: the organ
of pregnant wood hollow so with promise

of precarious stones south of Istanbul!
to sit by the Dardanelles, and to see

dead men push stones away, see them
raise the skull at the sound of water,
here. in the straits. south of Istanbul.

ORFEO, WITH HIS LUTE

and underneath the mango tree
me honey and I
will make woo-loo-loo

the smell of pomade still lurks,
like grief quarantined,
in this tin cup of valentino-silk,
imported from Portugal
once, and left behind now,
as if to no end, a mere
surplus of meaning in ghosts.

II

to think so is easy
on bitter days,
full of crossroads and forks;

to think, too,
of carefree women whom love
touched into grace in Venice,

and to think too
the gondolier's pole slides
in so to work the tight canals of Venice
the smell of juice and rot.

III

but to have caught, even once,
at the sun's gold body!
to have made laughter with men
when some other wall bends to lose its city!

IV

there are worse things to be
kept at bay; behind a line of yellow windows:

in the letter the woman sits
to write; when she takes a razor
to the wounded heart; and makes it
an urgent thing to surrender
then and be nothing
of herself that remains of you.

V

there is an eyeless beggar in Flaubert
grace-enchanted; self-regarding
and touched so:

with his body given back to him
in the loud noise of himself in his clogs;
in the clatter of himself in his sticks.

enchanted, he sang into himself
such chansons of me and mine!
of petticoats and of thighs he thought
the hand forever ready to reach
into, to meet as if to no end
of meaning, as if to no end
at all; as if the heart, in all things,
        remains. unmoored.

CALYPSO FOR CALIBAN

ackee rice salt fish is nice

as when I set down to substance
and to sum, but, seduced, think
to be elf with printless foot
is admiration and nice

this is the place
my inheritance
a chain of leached bones
my inheritance
mother this
chain of leached stones
airless quays
dust that rises
to coast on water

but they walk on water
for you
they walk on water
papa prospero
atibo legba
the whores
with water will
walk on water

papa prospero
jig me mama
an' jig she mama
papa prospero jig
jig me mama
to born the beast

prospero
atibo legba
is him goin to make
all and thee
prosperous so;

to make the beast
is him goin to kiss
in his own true-true name
the whores
until the red part white
more so than black can
white in she certain parts.

Mary-Miranda and mother
and holy virgin,
so come to us
so pray for us
in all your own
true-true name—that the will
be done too for dem mamas with
the derelict vaginas,
though defunct; that they be
holy maid and ready
now to make the beast
with atibo prospero
even till the kingdom.
come, keep the air
out of Sycorax hole:

let this, that I am
set to be, choke unborn
where she think to born
me black; lacking
in air that is light,

for is so things happen,
papa prospero,
if a whore put
to black lips, sir,
on her private vagina, sir.

but, you, virgin
daughter of god's
own true self,
admired so in

your body's own self,
keep open the carnival,
this feast of ashes,
and Lent (this dance
of flex knee
and tight thigh)
for when the black
beast to come
prowls so about
the derelict pasture
that is man's
braincase sometimes;

when I will prowl
these quays,
dissatisfied, with my face
prospero
against the face
prospero
of your daughter
prospero
prowling the fringes
of the tempest.

god's own daughter,
ora pro nobis,
and again be admired

when I turn the corners
of these my eyes
for a vision of hulks
and black flesh
drugged in vomit and fart,
ora pro nobis

when I set down to substance
and to sum and think to be
elf with printless foot
is admiration and nice;

when, the wind breaks
in derelict places,
and I grow to be at last
not ariel-spirit
not daughter-flesh,
but prey for us,

be present at the table,
and in your own
true-true admiration
when I am myself again
only in this or that corner
of a dissatisfied face;

        be present
while and still I am ready,
if the revel end,
to wake and cry to dream again.

CIRCULAR RUINS

The Message That Failed
God sent the chameleon to humans with the message that they should have eternal life, and the lizard with the message that they must die. On the way, the chameleon lallygagged, the chameleon lallygagged so, and the lizard arrived first. When she had delivered her message, the matter was settled.

THE IDEA OF JUMPING

a span of bridges makes discovery
of water a delay; works
a hardship of hope in a bundle
that looks to tumble well,
and beyond the arc's parenthesis and reach.

a bridge too far cheats the cove
below, where the body settles,
beyond itself, in water and stone.

SUFI: TARIGA

in the ear, where small bones hold
the earth to the promise of a centre,

there is only one step, no more,
to the dance of a whirling dervish.

WITH A KNIFE OR A RAZOR BLADE...

it is *for* initiates
that blood roots
back so into itself;

that it conjures up more
than is enough
of cold prodigies out of the sea.

shot now from below the sky
the sun lies, a well,
and blood-red in its bowline:

the razor edge bleeds under the belly
of the chalk-marked girls with breasts
—that seed may grow—
the foreskin hangs its knife-red blow
in the cupped hands of initiates.

sacrifice given, sacrifice accepted.

even so...
to look unblinking at the moon,
to see mooncold prodigies as these
are from over the left shoulder,
is to know the failed economies of pain
mid-scream, and the urge not to live.

FUNERAL RITES

rien de rien

by force of habit provocative
with habit and hope,
Don Juan plays the gigolo,
and still, to stony rubbish in hell,

certain as certain is sure
death never comes
in at a wrong door.

though our deaths are forever
profligate with heartbeat and ache,
the cracks are too antiquely
lit to be ill-behaved so.

how else should I think
but pianissimo, nostalgique,
and regret nothing of Piaf?

she who, milord, died so
as to be nothing of nothing,
to be done with the lay;
even if by habit, and by stroke
of luck, still, Don Juan plays gigolo
down even to stony rubbish.

THE GROWING OF GRAPES

in the beginning everything was,
true, water and dark. though
layer upon layer of habitation
will yield to teasing:

like lapis lazuli and stibium
on the dead eyes of a dead woman
only dead for sure in Memphis.

or a caravanserei returns, loping,
to Basra in damask and taffeta
with mother of pearls, inlaid
for the knife.

chicken bones on bought plates,
with wide laughter in a mouth
that waits to burn
at Herculaneum; the hot anxious
struggle of grapes to grow.
and Vesuvius, above it so, rising,
impolitic so as stone.

BELLADONNA

He wanted to dream a man, he wanted to dream him in
minute entirety, and impose him on reality.
—Jorge Luís Borges, "The Circular Ruins"

A touch or two of belladonna to the eye
and every country gains
in darkness and believable weight.

but if, like Polyphemus, you lose
even the eyeball, then
smell out where the night remains
and is godfat for no man's agony.

then ask Creon (we must think
to ask Creon in his high knowledge
of dead bodies) where the land
benefits in a woman passionate for dust.

ARMISTICE

*He said, I did not know that weeping over the
ruins of old buildings could be so painful.*
    -Edwar al-Kharat, *City of Saffron*

The train whistles its way past the hot lizards
on the plateau at Jos;
we cross the bridge near Kafanchan

below, on the *Moghoya Dji*, the paddles
of wooden steamers break
up bamboo and lotus on water

bright water falls from the loin cloths
of crab fishermen; catching the sun

at Kaduna, indigo tunics have left their dyes
on the breasts of long-nippled women.

they wave; the train speeds. the wheels
shatter hard coals about our eyes, and the smell
of iron and rough ashes breaks into our nostrils.

the trains speeds; we have put
cut sandalwood on these coffins we carry
north to their rest and to ours.

the earths drifts on, its way
always between contamination and cure.

NOTES

Pages

8   **Epigaph:** from "Wisdom"—as translated in *Classic Black African Poems*, ed.Willard Trask.

8   **Ngoni Litany:** collected and translated in *Ants Will Not Eat Your Fingers,* ed. Leonard Doob.

21   **Houses of Mole:** the vernacular landscape and inspiration are traditional Dogon, as reproduced in, say, **African Arts** magazine (UCLA).

36   In **XLV,** especially, *Sally in our alley* and *Tom Pierce* are among several English songs that made up the repertoire of Freetown's secondary school choirs, in the 1950s.

39   **Spengler:** During World War I Oswald Spengler, the philosopher, as will the Nazi propaganda Magazine *Signal,* in World War II, made a point of emphasizing the "black peril" involved in France's use of "colored" races to protect her culture. For report on Spengler interview, see Ramon Guirao, *Orbita de la poesia afrocubana.*

39   **warum sagen sie "fromage"?** (german): why do you say "fromage"? (french word for "cheese")— asked in mock(?) puzzlement of French-speaking African soldiers.

39   **Adam in the presence** and **Peter, go ring da bell** are Krio *shouts.*